*Overcoi*

# Sham

# Overcoming Shame and Guilt

## *Step By Step Guide On How to Overcome Shame and Guilt for Good*

**Antony Felix**

# Your Free Gift

As a way of thanking you for the purchase, I'd like to offer you a complimentary gift:

- **5 Pillar Life Transformation Checklist:** This short book is about life transformation, presented in bit size pieces for easy implementation. I believe that without such a checklist, you are likely to have a hard time implementing anything in this book and any other thing you set out to do religiously and sticking to it for the long haul. It doesn't matter whether your goals relate to weight loss, relationships, personal finance, investing, personal development, improving communication in your family, your overall health, finances, improving your sex life, resolving issues in your relationship, fighting PMS successfully, investing, running a successful business, traveling etc. With a checklist like this one, you can bet that anything you do will seem a lot easier to implement until the end. Therefore, even if you don't continue reading this book, at least read the one thing that will help you in every other aspect of your life. Grab your copy now by clicking/tapping here or simply enter http://bit.ly/2fantonfreebie into your browser. Your life will never be the same again (if you implement what's in this book), I promise.

**PS:** I'd like your feedback. If you are happy with this book, please leave a review on Amazon.

# Introduction

*"With everything that has happened to you, you can either feel sorry for yourself or treat what has happened as a gift. Everything is either an opportunity to grow or an obstacle to keep you from growing. You get to choose."*

Wayne W. Dyer

Life as we know it is a series of experiences, some good, some not so good. When the "good" happens, we rejoice, treasure the memories, and repeatedly relive their glorious delight. Unfortunately, when the "bad" happens, which it so often does, instead of treasuring the experience for what it is, a lesson meant to fuel our development and growth, many of us choose to beat ourselves up for our "perceived" shortcomings.

By beating ourselves up, we cultivate two highly charged, and possibly negative—depending on your perception and reaction—emotions: **shame** and **guilt**, both of which in their extremes are a burdensome load to carry.

Since our reaction to all manners of stimuli determines our feelings towards it, to manage shame and guilt, we need to exercise control over our emotional and physical reactions to all circumstances. As Wayne Dyer puts it, emotional control, and therefore the ability to manage and overcome guilt and shame, is a personal choice: "you can choose to see everything as *either an opportunity to grow or an obstacle to keep you from growing. You get to choose."*

This guide is about dealing with, and triumphing over shame and guilt. The aim of this guide is to help you understand how you perceive and react to "seemingly bad or negative" situations or circumstances (which is where shame and guilt develop), and to tweak your reactions so that you curtail the development of shame and guilt as burdensome emotions.

Let's begin!

# Table of Contents

**Your Free Gift** _____ 2

**Introduction** _____ 3

**Section 1: Guilt and Shame 101: Everything You Need To Know** _____ 8

**Chapter 1: Understanding Shame and Guilt** 8

**Chapter 2: Common Misconceptions about Shame, Embarrassment, and Guilt** _____ 15

*Shame and embarrassment are the same; they are not* _____ 16

*Shame is bad; it is not Always Bad*_____ 18

*Shame and Guilt are the same thing; they are not* _____ 20

**Chapter 3: Shame as a Negative Emotion, How We Express it, & Why We Feel It** _____ 23

*How We Express Shame* _____ 25

*Why We Feel Shame (and Guilt in Extension)* _ 26

**Chapter 4: Different Kinds of Guilt** _____ 29

**Section 2: Your Guide to Overcoming Shame and Guilt** _____ 35

**Chapter 5: How to Handle Shame (In a Productive Way)** _____35

**Chapter 6: How to Deal with Toxic, Unhealthy Guilt**_____52

**Conclusion** _____64

**Do You Like My Book & Approach To Publishing?** _____66

*1: First, I'd Love It If You Leave a Review of This Book on Amazon.*_____66

*2: Check Out My Emotional Mastery Books ____66*

*3: Grab Some Freebies On Your Way Out; Giving Is Receiving, Right?* _____67

**PSS: Let Me Also Help You Save Some Money!** _____68

**Copyright 2019 by Fantonpublishers.com - All rights reserved.**

# Section 1: Guilt and Shame 101: Everything You Need To Know

# Chapter 1: Understanding Shame and Guilt

To overcome shame (and guilt), you need to understand each individually.

## Shame

The term shame comes from an Old English Word hama, a word whose literal meaning is "covering or veiling up." Wikipedia defines shame as

*"An unpleasant self-conscious emotion typically associated with a negative evaluation of the self, withdrawal motivations, and feelings of distress, exposure, mistrust, powerlessness, and worthlessness."*

Shame relates to how we feel about ourselves while guilt relates to awareness of how our actions affect others in injurious ways.

Shame is our least favorite feeling. In fact, many researchers believe it is our most painful emotion. We experience shame as a feeling of "worthlessness." As you will later learn, shame is a healthy emotion, which is why the goal of this guide is not to help you eliminate shame (or guilt), but to help you manage and control it so that is does not turn into intense shame or guilt, the kind that makes you feel bad or not good enough, and that lead to an altered, negative state that is not conducive to your wellbeing.

Intense shame is exactly that, an intense emotion. When intense shame leads to an altered state, an unhealthy mental and physical state where we feel unworthy, we retreat into ourselves because of which our interpersonal relationships suffer and we feel stuck in a vortex of negativity. When experienced long enough, intense shame has the tendency to turn into a negative character trait, which is why shame can be both a trait and a state.

## Guilt

Guilt is a developmental achievement that comes about when we do something "bad" that we feel remorseful for doing—so much so that we would like to make amends for the offense. Unlike shame, when we are experiencing guilt, we do not believe we are "bad" per se, we just believe that we have done "something wrong." Feeling guilty often leads to the desire for penance, which can be anything such as doing something to repair a broken relation.

The main difference between shame and guilt is that one focuses on the self (shame) while the other (guilt) focuses on the action. Because of this difference, how we respond to shame and guilt varies depending on the stimulation.

Because guilt emphasizes the action, feeling guilt in healthy doses is a good thing.

Guilt primarily relates to our beliefs of what we consider moral or immoral, right or wrong. When something violates our sense of morality, guilt is the resulting emotion we experience.

Compared to shame, guilt is a bit healthier because it breeds a desire to do something to right a wrong or an attempt to fix a problem. When comparing shame, embarrassment, and guilt, we often note that shame has a strong emphasis on the self, our self-image or how we view or perceive ourselves. Shame has an inwardly focus, which is why experiencers of intense shame feel unworthy and incapable of taking action towards the relief of the altered state brought on by intense shame.

Shame is a belief of "I am bad because I did a bad thing." Guilt, on the other hand, is a sentiment of "I did a bad thing that I feel remorseful for. Doing a bad thing does not mean I am a bad person. I just did something others or I consider "below a set of personal and social standards of what I/we consider moral or immoral, right or wrong."

Shame is also a state of inner conflict, a discrepancy in our self-image vis-à-vis the aims of our ego self and a set of personal and societal standards. Intense levels of shame have the ability to impair psychological functioning. For instance, many disorders such as eating disorders, social disorders and narcissism, the ultimate defense against an internal and external sense of shame, have a strong shame element.

Unlike shame, we experience guilt (ego-syntonic) when our self-image and the goals and needs of our ego self are consistent and in agreement. Guilt in healthy doses is great for personal development. However, when left unchecked, it can lead to the development of an inferiority complex, a negative self-image that signals poor psychological functionality.

Depending on the circumstance, shame is likely to lead to a negative self-image—a negative self-image is one of the hallmark traits of shame—while guilt is likely to be a standout trait of high self-esteem especially in relation to the ability to recognize mistakes and then take actions towards their rectification. When we feel guilty, we are likely to want to take restitutive measures. On the other hand, shame, thanks to its internal focus, is likely to lead to negative self-talk, which at its barest is rumination, thinking negative thoughts.

Pervasive or intense shame keeps the positive feelings of remorse, concern, and guilt from taking root in the personality. This leads to a deeper sense of feeling worthless or damaged.

Shame impedes growth while experiencing guilt can act as a growth catalyst. Experiencing guilt is as painful as experiencing shame. However, since guilt is cognizance of the hurtful nature of our actions and behaviors, it is more positive and growth-driven in the sense that experiencing it can make experiencing empathy easier. Empathy then leads to feelings of remorse and a desire to "ease the pain" caused.

Shame tends to lead to negative behavior; on the other hand, guilt can be the catalyst for positive change in our behavior and self-image. When using guilt as a tool for positive change, it is important to be cautious because it is also possible to use guilt to influence good or bad change.

Guilt is also helpful as a conflict prevention tool; when there is a moral code, shame and guilt are the resulting emotions when something we are doing or are about to do fails to align with this moral code. Guilt promotes good behaviors and relations (our moral codes).

### Guilt vs Shame

I did something bad          I am bad

Next, let's demystify some misconceptions about shame, embarrassment, and guilt.

# Chapter 2: Common Misconceptions about Shame, Embarrassment, and Guilt

That shame and embarrassment are the same thing is a common misconception. Even though the emotions tend to have great overlaps in the way we experience and express them, they are not the same.

# Shame and embarrassment are the same; they are _not_

Embarrassment is a sense of momentary discomfort experienced when we feel vulnerable, i.e. when we feel as if an aspect of ourselves—our self-image specifically—is under threat of exposure in a way that undermines the positive self-image we project within our social circle and society in general.

Causes of embarrassment change according to circumstances—and the company in question—with most forms of embarrassment emanating from simple behaviors such as farting or belching, to presumably actions and behaviors such as an oafish partner, a rude child or associate.

Like embarrassment, it is possible to experience vicarious shame, i.e. to feel shame because of someone's deeds, actions, or behaviors especially when the person in question is someone with whom you have close relations.

Unlike embarrassment, shame is our response to something we consider morally disgraceful or wrong. Unlike embarrassment, shame can attach itself to actions and thoughts that remain underneath the surface, hidden from our social circles.

Shame and embarrassment are intense emotional responses. Shame, however, is deeper and more manifest (internally) partly because it emanates not just from our social image or character, but also from how we relate to our moral character.

A key difference between shame and embarrassment is that shame lacks an element of public humiliation while embarrassment has one especially in the form of social awkwardness, a non-severe and mild form of shame. Another key difference is that shame is internal and often experienced privately while embarrassment is more public.

# Shame is bad; it is *not* Always Bad

Although shame is not one of the seven basic emotions we have innately at birth, it is essential to our wellbeing, which is why it is a healthy emotion, one we do not want to eliminate altogether.

Here are the main reasons why shame and guilt in healthy doses is good for you and for your wellbeing:

### 1: *It illuminates our vulnerabilities*

Chronic shame manifests internally as the beliefs we have about ourselves. To some degree, this kind of shame can be essential because when we learn to look out for it and handle it in a healthy manner, it allows us to face up to our vulnerabilities, and from this internal self-awareness, develop a growth minded focus on what we perceive to be our weaknesses.

### 2: *Shame is good for your ego*

Shame and guilt are ego-deflators; they are an intense feeling of "feeling wronged or feeling you have wronged others." A great example of this is how we can experience shame and guilt when we do something externally hurtful or feel ashamed when someone calls us out (feeling morally ashamed).

How we perceive our emotions is more important than the emotions themselves. When we are self-aware enough to perceive shame positively, all forms of shame can be positive. For instance, doing something that violates your values can be a catalyst for growth.

### *3: It's a sort of compliment*

Shame falls under a category of compliments called "backhand compliments, a term The Collin's Dictionary defines as "a remark that at first glance looks like an insult but looked at closely, can also be complimentary and vice versa."

Feeling shame is only possible when you are self-aware, and therefore self-conscious, both of which are essential to personal development. Feeling bad (guilty) because you have done something wrong or awful is a great indicator of remorse and guilt, both of which when handled positively, can be great for your wellbeing and personal growth.

Experiencing healthy amounts of shame indicates you are a decent human being. Deconstructing your shame (and guilt) and understanding its triggers can bring about personal growth because shame and guilt show us our existing and perceived weaknesses, many of which we can work on and improve thus bringing about a positive self-image.

# Shame and Guilt are the same thing; they are _not_

Even though they are different psychological emotions, the common use of the terms embarrassment, shame, and guilt is interchangeable in society.

We feel shame when we feel in violation of cultural or personal values. We feel guilt when an occurrence violates our inner values.

Shame focuses on the self: evaluating ourselves negatively. When we are experiencing guilt, the "self," our internal and external self, is not central to the narrative. Unlike shame that focuses on self-punishment for perceived wrongdoings, guilt focuses on the offense. When we are feeling guilty of something we did to offend someone, we are feeling responsible and regretful of the situation.

The *'feeling responsible'* element is important because when you feel responsible for something, you are likely to want to make restitution by taking specific, growth-minded actions. Since it focuses more on the inner person and less on the offence, shame, is a likely cause of self-hate, a negative self-image, bodily tensions, and daily chronic stress and anxiety.

A key difference between shame, embarrassment, and guilt is that shame does not explicitly involve a sense of public humiliation, a key element in embarrassment, which is why it is possible to feel shame for an ingrained, internal sense of 'unworthiness.' To feel embarrassed or guilty, your behaviors and actions must have an external element such as "appearing worthless socially or wronging others."

Another key difference between shame, embarrassment, and guilt is the intensity of the experience. Feeling embarrassed is equal to experiencing a light, functional, and adaptive sense of shame. On the other hand, intense and toxic shame is dysfunctional, negative, and debilitating to our wellbeing. The difference between functional and dysfunctional shame is *its intensity and our reaction to the stimuli.*

Shame can be heteronomous, externally driven by others, or autonomous, coming from our internal self-image. It can also be a natural response to internal and external conditioning. Chronic shame is also a self-esteem issue emanating from a poor self-image. Intense shame is often a result of judging ourselves harshly or imagining how others will judge us harshly if they discover something we consider "shameful."

Unlike guilt that often leads to a supplicating action or behavior—driven by a sense of "responsibility"—when we feel shamed or ashamed, we are likely to defend ourselves, which breeds contempt and leads to deeper shame, a state that when left unchecked, can encumber your wellbeing and progress in life.

In the next chapter, we will focus on shame as a negative emotion, how we express it as well as why we feel it.

# Chapter 3: Shame as a Negative Emotion, How We Express it, & Why We Feel It

How we relate to shame is what gives it a negative power over how we feel and relate with ourselves and with others. At the most basic level, shame is a basic emotion whose social or moral connotation can cause a desire to "deny (or hide) what we consider to be our wrongdoings."

Chronic shame, the kind that leads to an altered state, is a result of negative self-evaluation, a negative self-image emanating from carrying shame and the resonating guilt until it alters your internal and external perception and character. When you are feeling intensely 'shameful,' you are comparing your actions or behaviors to a set of internal and external standards and upon finding discrepancies, blaming yourself for the inadequacies, "feeling worthless and blaming yourself for the perceived worthlessness."

When we experience chronic shame (remember that shame can also be good and healthy), our focus is internal. Negative shame focuses on who we are a person: how we identify with ourselves, which is why negative shame is self-punishment for our perceived failings or shortcomings. When you are in a state of intense shame, you are likely to feel victimized by internal or external stimuli.

We express shame, i.e. a sense of shame, as feeling guilty (consciously feeling bad about how we, for example, wronged someone,) or subconsciously as an awareness of our innate need to exercise restraint in instances where our behaviors and actions can appear offensive to others (the sense of being modest or humble).

# How We Express Shame

When we experience profound shame, we use a covering gesture such as a downcast gaze or a slacking posture.

Depending on the type of shame experienced, how ingrained it is, and the effect it has on other emotions and actions, "feeling shame" can also be in the form of analysis paralysis, an inability to make decisions and take decisive action, mental stress and confusion, brain fog, body and muscular aches, pains, and tension.

Worth noting is that as long as you are living and therefore making mistakes and learning from them, you cannot live life without experiencing a form of shame. For this reason, our aim is not to eliminate shame (or guilt) altogether but to learn how to cope with, and use both as catalysts for positive change in our lives.

# Why We Feel Shame (and Guilt in Extension)

Why we feel shame and guilt comes from four key components of our being.

We feel shame (and guilt) because:

## 1: Self-awareness

Without self-awareness, it would be impossible to experience shame or guilt. Awareness in this sense means internal awareness and external awareness.

Shame, or to "cover up" is the fleeting or ingrained fear of being in the spotlight where your "shortcomings" will become more pronounced especially when said 'shortcomings' do not align with a set of standard or personal values.

When you are aware, you know of a specific set of internal and external standards meant to guide your decisions of what is right or wrong. Self-awareness is a prerequisite to learning how to deal with shame and guilt in a positive, growth-minded way.

## 2: A sense of responsibility

Shame leads to self-blame, a focus on the self rather than on the stimulation or object of shame. When we are feeling vulnerable, it is easy to assess a situation in a manner that leads to self-blame, where because we are feeling responsible, to blame, we are likely to feel ashamed or guilty for action or behaviors we consider contravening our values and accepted social norms.

## 3: Standards

Your standards relate to your beliefs towards specific emotions, feelings, thoughts, and action. They form out of your belief system, what you believe to be acceptable and true on a personal and social level.

An example of this is the standard belief that in some instances such as a funeral, expressing joy in any form leads to a sense of shame—because laughter in this case would seem to indicate "gladness in the death."

Another apt example of how shame develops from personal and societal standards relates to how in some communities, leaving dog turds on the sidewalk is a cause for shame and guilt to dog owners.

## 4: Personal traits

Being self-conscious makes you prone to shame and guilt. A tendency to avoid shame also leads to deeper shame and a likeliness to blame others as a way to avoid self-blame and the resulting sense of responsibility that leads to remorse and guilt.

Self-esteem, a key aspect of our personality traits, also influences the sense and experience of shame and guilt. What you feel towards yourself, your attitude towards your weaknesses and capabilities, can determine the kind of, and intensity of shame and guilt you experience.

When you think of yourself as "unworthy," your internal dialog and self-image is negative, and because you have a poorly developed self-image, you are likely to take things personally, or label yourself as 'bad' more often.

Let's now discuss the different kinds that exist.

# Chapter 4: Different Kinds of Guilt

Depending on the kind of guilt experienced and the intensity of the experience, guilt can act as a catalyst for positive change. Guilt has three main sub types: **natural guilt**, **toxic guilt**, and **existential guilt**.

Natural guilt is a common, natural occurrence experienced by all. Toxic guilt is the kind of guilt you do not want to lug around. This kind of guilt is negative and detrimental to your wellbeing, which is why you have to learn to let it go or use it as a catalyst for positive change and growth.

We shall now engage in a brief discussion on how to deal with the different types of guilt. Later, we shall discuss how to handle toxic guilt and use guilt positively, as a catalyst for personal growth and development.

## 1: Natural guilt

We can define natural guilt as remorse or regret over our actions or behaviors. This type of guilt is very definitive and specific to a certain incident. For instance, lying to a loved one—good intentioned or not—can be a cause for remorse.

Natural guilt is very healthy and relative to specific actions and behaviors, which is why this type of guilt focuses less on "feeling bad internally" to "feeling remorseful or responsible for the effect of the decisions and actions you have taken."

Natural guilt also tends to be present oriented, i.e. you are likely to experience it locally and shortly after the 'offending' incident; lying to a partner about where you were is a great example of localized, natural guilt.

Even though natural guilt is healthy, its experience is mentally and to a lesser degree, physically painful and trying especially when our behaviors and actions (or lack thereof) lead to serious relational damage with the involved parties.

Unlike most forms of guilt, local guilt it always easy to handle and use for personal growth. For instance, when doing something bad or hurtful leads to a deep sense of regret or remorse, it is easy to implement counter measures such as a solid explanation or a heartfelt and genuine apology and plea for forgiveness—and the subsequent change of behavior.

The easiest way to dissolve natural guilt is by doing something that repairs the damage caused by specific behaviors and actions. Since local guilt is a natural part of our nervous system, the goal is not to eliminate it altogether. The goal is to use it as a sort of alarm system that allows us to recognize behaviors and actions that fail to align with our internal and external moral code and values, and when these behaviors occur, to take action towards behavioral change and self-improvement.

Developing your empathic abilities, the aspect of being able to put yourself in someone's situation or shoes, is one of the best ways to develop a deep sense of natural guilt and to use guilt constructively. When you can empathize with someone's situation or suffering, it becomes easier to see errors in your behaviors and action, and to take specific actions that rectify your mistakes, thereby easing the sense of guilt long before it festers and develops into toxic guilt.

Work towards creating a personal relationship with natural guilt so that when you experience it, instead of agonizing over it, which is how toxic guilt develops, you can do something productive with it; perhaps use it as an impetus for behavioral change.

A great example of this is in the form of dealing with the guilt we are likely to experience when we commit ourselves to something, such as promising to call someone, but then fail to fulfill our part of the commitment. In such a case, the easiest way to deal with the distilled sense of natural guilt is to offer an explanation or tender an apology perhaps by calling the person and explaining the situation.

Although natural guilt is beneficial, it also has an ugly side where someone can guilt you into doing something or behaving a specific way (manipulation through guilt). This is very common in religions, relationships, and even modern day societies. Natural guilt turns corrosive when used for control or as a form of punishment.

Dealing with natural guilt is a lesson in self-compassion (and being compassionate towards others). How do you becoming better at practicing compassion towards others as well as towards yourself?

The easiest strategy by which to become more compassionate is to start practicing it with those closest to you: yourself and your loved ones. Say, for example, something you do ends up being hurtful to a loved one. Being compassionate, i.e. practicing the act of being sympathetic to someone's feelings, can help you recognize the level of pain you have inflicted. This realization is then likely to lead to actions meant to ease the degree of pain (and in consequence, the level of guilt you experience).

## 2: Toxic guilt

Toxic guilt is "prolonged, healthy guilt." When healthy guilt becomes ingrained, it breeds a negative self-image; on its part, a negative self-image leads to behavioral, unconscious patterns that lead to the development of deep-rooted guilt and shame.

Since it develops out of behavioral patterns, toxic guilt is more challenging to handle, which is why the best approach is to take strategic actions that turn it into natural, easy-to-handle guilt.

Since this type of shame is unhealthy, our aim is to learn how to handle it in a positive way, which a later chapter talks about at length. Before that, keep in mind that no matter how careful you are in your interactions, feeling guilty (and shameful) is unavoidable because as you live your life, you will make mistakes that hurt others, or take actions that contravene your values and beliefs. That is Ok and is part of our human nature.

## 3: Existential guilt

Although existential, i.e. relating to our community and our existence in it, existential guilt is both painful and reasonable because as long as you are living, it is impossible to live in harmony with all things—living or otherwise—, laws, or cultural beliefs and values. As long as you are breathing and living, you will have a negative effect on others including the various elements in your environment.

The most potent remedy for existential guilt is an unconditional offering, "to give 'something' to life as a thank you for its many offerings and blessings." The easiest way to practice this is to practice being grateful for your blessings and many privileges and by doing something that benefits the society in which you live.

Existential guilt is very often a byproduct of feeling "out of control, a strong sense of social wrong but a perceived inability to do something about it." In measured dosages, existential guilt is good because it increases your internal and external awareness, making you a more balanced human being.

Other than practicing gratitude, unconditional offering, and playing your part in the betterment of the society in which you live, being compassionate (instead of self-sacrificial) is another great way to overcome this type of shame.

Another remedy for existential guilt is the nature of the world. You have influence over a very small part of the environment in which you live. Accepting that you can only do so much to change your existence or environment is a great way to free yourself from the claws of negative existential guilt.

Yes, you should do your part to make society better—the guilt you feel should lead to some form of action—but in general though, feeling guilty for things outside your control is nothing short of a personal disservice and punishment. You may not be able to do much to end war, hunger, or poverty; do what is within your control—what you can—and then simply let the guilt of what you are unable to do pass over you.

Next, our focus will be how to overcome shame and guilt.

# Section 2: Your Guide to Overcoming Shame and Guilt

# Chapter 5: How to Handle Shame (In a Productive Way)

We shall discuss steps and strategies that when implemented should help you let go of and deal with any type of shame, even shame that may be keeping you from achieving your full potential.

## Step #1: A & I (be Aware and Identify)

A & I stand for Awareness and Identifying, which are the first steps towards letting go of shame for good and in a productive manner.

Awareness in this case means becoming aware enough to identify the cause of shame. As noted earlier, shame can be internal, emanating from behavioral thought patterns, or external, emanating from specific circumstances and situations.

To become aware enough to identify the triggering causes of your sense of shame requires asking yourself important questions. Which shame-related messages do you replay often? How do these messages and thought patterns affect your wellbeing as well as that of others? How does experiencing shame (and guilt in extension) make you feel? Is there something you can do about it in the present? The more you introspect, the easier it shall be to practice self-awareness, to identify the triggers, and to feel positive enough to want to do something about it right now.

Being aware of and able to identify shame (the experience) is especially important because among other things, it allows you to reconnect with one of the core principle of being human: we are imperfect, *because of which we are prone to making all manners of mistakes.*

Expecting perfection—from others as well as from yourself—is unrealistic and likely to lead to a decreased sense of self-esteem/worth—which is likely to lead to shame, elements of guilt, low self-confidence, and many other psychosomatic disorders.

Let go of ideas of what you "should" do or how you should be in specific circumstances such as social constructs that when followed, drive us towards seeking perfectionism, and feeling shame and guilt when we fall short of these expectations. By developing a healthy sense of self, it becomes easier to recognize instances that can bring on shame, to label shame when it occurs, and to direct it towards constructive avenues such as constructive criticism.

How can you practice awareness and your ability to identify when you are experiencing shame?

Here are two key ways:

## **Journaling**

Get into the habit of journaling your thoughts at the start and end of each day. Research has shown that writing down your feelings and emotions can have a cathartic effect on your wellbeing.

When you get into the habit of writing down what you are feeling and experiencing in your day-to-day life, it gives you a chance to relate with your emotions in a way that is both friendly to your sanity and good for your personal development.

Journal your expectation at the start of the day and at day's end, your thoughts about the day that was (or is about to end). Dedicate at least 10-15 minutes to doing this. Additionally, whenever you are dealing with an intense sense of shame, write down your thoughts about the situation causing the shame and as you do, ask yourself deep questions: why do I feel this way? What situation caused this sense of shame? Is the shame internally or externally driven? Is there something I can do about it right now?

Asking yourself such questions allows your mind to relate what you are feeling to the circumstances that make up your daily life and to identify the triggers for all your emotions including shame. It also gives you a deep sense of awareness, and when you are aware, you are a step away from instituting an effective remedy.

## ***Practice mindful meditation***

Mindfulness meditation is the ultimate self-awareness tool. When you make its practice habitual in your daily life, it allows you to focus your attention to the present moment. The effects of focusing on the present moment are astronomical.

For one, when you remain focused on the present moment, you remain aware of your mind as it courts and flirts with thoughts, feelings, and emotions from one minute to the next. Because intense shame has a strong internal focus, i.e. "feeling ashamed to a point where you feel unworthy," when you practice mindfulness and become present oriented, it allows you to 'catch and change' negative thoughts and perceptions long before they turn into a negative self-image or the need to berate yourself for perceived shortcomings.

The essence of mindfulness meditation for effective shame (and guilt) relief is to become an explorer of your thoughts and of your inner self. Practiced consistently, mindfulness meditation will help you become aware of, and able to identify shame experienced in the moment or shame that you have buried deep inside you and that you have been avoiding.

Here is how to go about the practice:

1. Adopting a comfortable posture while in a calm and serene environment is a key element in all forms of meditation. In this case, sit or lie down comfortably. If you choose to sit, sit straight with the curvature of your back maintained (not tensed), palms on your laps, and feet firmly planted on the ground. If you choose to lie down, lie down comfortably but not too comfortably that you drift off to sleep. Set a timer for 10-20 minutes and begin the formal practice.

2. Once settled into your posture, close your eyes and bring your attention to the body as you sit or lie down. Pay attention to how the body contacts with the chair, the floor, or the bed—whatever surface you are sitting or lying on. Soften your body, allowing your shoulders, jaw, back, and trunk of the body to reset and rest easy. Take a few deep, diaphragmatic breaths and on the count of five, let your breath return to normal.

3. Turn your attention to your breathing and start noticing where you feel it the most. Does the in-breath appear

more pronounced at the nostril, chest, or belly level? Notice everything you can notice about the in and out breath and especially pay attention to the sensations brought on by this automatic habit. Practice watching your breath for a while (2-5 minutes is enough) and when you feel calm and relaxed enough, shift your attention to the state of your mind.

4.  Become attentive to your mind and the going-on in there. Notice the thoughts present in your mind at this precise moment and take a moment to appreciate them. Do not try to change your thoughts; simply observe them and let them be for now. Shift your attention back and form between your thoughts and your breath. After practicing this for a while, focus your attention on your shame sentiments.

5.  Think of an instance that is causing you shame—it could be a fresh memory or a shameful memory you have held on to for a while. Turn towards that experience or situation and as you do so, monitor your thoughts, feelings, emotions, sentiments towards the situation; also notice the bodily sensations experienced as you relive the shame mentally. Do not attempt to change or control anything; simply watch and explore all thoughts and emotions arising in the present. Identify, name, and label all thoughts and emotions arising as a result. When you notice shame, name it as so; when you notice guilt or fear, name them as so; when you notice remorse, name it as so,

and continue observing your mental and emotional state to the best of your abilities.

6. As you become more aware of the sensations associated with your feelings, investigate them with curiosity and friendly interest; dedicate this moment to knowing your sensations and emotions (as well as yourself) as much as possible.

7. When you notice the sense of shame giving rise to strong mental and physical conditions and sensations, stop for a moment and say to yourself, "All emotions are neither good or bad; how I perceive them is what makes them so. The shameful and painful sensations I am feeling right now are fleeting moments of difficulty," and then refocus either on your breath or on observing thoughts and sensations as they come and go. Practice this for a while and if the mind wanders off to something unrelated to the aim of this practice, re-tether your attention to your breath and continue the observation.

8. With the sensation of shame (experienced emotional and physically) still in mind, start asking yourself, "how can I let go of this or let it be?" "Should I address this and how can I do so in a healthy manner?" "How can I change my attitude towards this situation—the shame causing situation—and see it in a more positive light?" Continue asking yourself such growth-minded question for the remainder of your meditation session, accepting things as they are. Once done, open your eyes, take in a deep

breath, and as you exhale, visualize all the shame you feel vacating your mind and body for good, and then go about your day mindfully.

When you practice this level of emotional and thought mindfulness in your daily life, you become aware and capable of identifying the main cause of shame (and guilt), and as we mentioned, self-awareness is a requisite to dealing with shame (and guilt).

## Action step

Start a journal and use it to pen down your thoughts—including those of shame and guilt—and your sentiments as you live your life. Also, start practicing mindfulness meditation for at least 5 minutes two times a day, in the morning and in the evening. These two practices will allow you to become aware enough to identify your emotional experiences and to learn how to treat emotions for the fleeting things they are, which will help them become more attuned to yourself and therefore capable of letting go of intense shame or guilt.

## Step #2: Practice self-compassion

Toxic shame (and guilt) are a byproduct of negative thought patterns and beliefs—rumination especially. Excessive rumination has shown to lead to self-loathing and increased amounts of shame and guilt. Some research material has shown a direct correlation between ruminating on thoughts of shame and depressive symptoms.

Self-compassion is the cure for rumination.

When you talk to yourself kindly—positive self-talk, the ultimate counter measure for negative self-talk, the source of rumination—it becomes easier to create a healthy sense of "SELF" and to see mistakes not as messages of your worthlessness as a person, but as a message of the need to practice self-kindness and self-growth.

Being compassionate towards yourself—and others—calls for the practice of present awareness/mindfulness, the ability to observe your self-talk, behaviors and actions from moment to moment, and to relate this to how you are treating yourself. And when you notice you are treating yourself unkindly, to relate that to how the negative thought pattern is affecting your wellbeing. You can practice self-compassion, showing yourself kindness, by journaling, visualization, affirmations, mantras, or through meditation.

On journaling, which we have discussed at length, at the very least, maintain a gratitude journal where you express your gratitude including being grateful for your thought-awareness, the ability to recognize when you are experiencing shame and all other manners of emotions.

Journaling is a liberating experience. Expressing your sentiments, "your secrets" on paper has a very healing effect that allows you to come to terms with the root cause of a large percentage of your feelings and emotions including the root cause of deeply rooted shame.

### Action step

Practice being kind and loving towards yourself; treat yourself as you would treat a dear friend or a child. Stop pursuing perfectionism, and seek the support of those who love and care for you. The Buddha was right when he said:

*"You yourself, as much as anybody in the entire universe deserve your love and affection."*

## Step #3: Develop shame resilience

As noted severally, intense shame—and guilt in extension—develop out of negative thought patterns. Being aware of your thoughts, able to identify negative thought patterns such as those related to shame, and to practice self-compassion is of such importance because it limits the power shame (and other emotions) has on you, and gives you greater control of how your emotions affect you (or how you respond to them).

After practicing being aware and from it, developing the ability to recognize the thought patterns related to shame, it pays to start debunking the shame. Debunking shame is the process of questioning the shame. The questioning can be in the form of important personal questions such as "what can I do better?" "How can I make this right?" "Why am I feeling shameful?"

Talking to your shame or speaking out your thoughts of shame is a very productive way by which to question your thoughts (even those of shame) in a productive manner that leads to self-growth.

Talking to your shame (and about your shame with loved ones, a support group, or a qualified professional) allows you to become more aware, which allows you to deal with the evoked feelings of shame as they arise. When you talk to your shame, it allows you to stop ruminating over it.

Talking about your shame with supportive people is an especially effective way to build shame resilience. When you talk about shame—perhaps by sharing your experience of a 'shaming event' with a loved one, a support group, or a professional—the effects are instantaneous: *you feel better, your anxiety decreases, and your self-talk brightens.*

Having a conversation about shame is not easy since shame is our least favorite feeling, one we are less likely to share and more likely to want to internalize and hide. *"Wanting to hide it"* is a very natural response to shame. In fact, shame is so prevalent an emotion because our default responses is to hide it. By hiding it instead of sharing it, we allow it to fester until it turns toxic and manifests as a deeply seated sense of worthlessness where you feel undeserving: undeserving of love, wealth, success, peace, happiness, etc.

Allowed to fester, shame has a tendency to develop into elements such as chronic depression, codependent behavior, and other negative life issues such as an unhealthy lifestyle— bad food choices and a lack of exercise.

On the other hand, when you welcome shame, acknowledge it, take heed of what it is trying to say, or share it with a support group, shame loses a large portion of its hold on you. This loss allows you to decouple from thoughts of "being bad—"I am bad" and to hitch your wagon to a positive sentiment such as "I did something bad or something bad happened," both of which are likely to lead to natural, healthy guilt, of which we shall talk about in later.

Developing resilience to shame allows you to detach from shame and shame beliefs that may be keeping you from living your best life. When negative thought patterns have a diminishing effect on your psyche, it becomes easier to practice self-compassion and to free yourself from shame and its deadly claws.

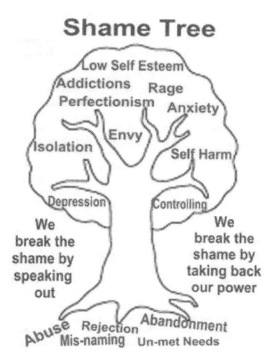

## How do you develop shame resilience?

Empathy is the easiest (and surest) method by which to develop shame resilience. Share your 'shameful' thoughts or sentiments with a trusted and supportive person such as a loved one or a professional therapist. Therapy is especially effective; by going through the therapy process—or just talking to someone who listens—you will experience a sense of empathy, feeling as if someone understand exactly what you are feeling, and because of this, you will be able to cultivate more empathy in your personal life and relationships.

## *Action step*

Find someone you can confide in, someone with whom you can share your thoughts, feelings, and emotions. If you lack such a person in your personal life, you can pour your pain and shame-thoughts within the pages of your journal, and if that is not enough, seek professional help.

## Step #4: Experience and express

Because we experience shame at varying intensities, how we react to it also varies. In some people, feeling ashamed leads to defensiveness, while in others, it leads to negative self-talk and in some extremes, self-loath.

The need to experience your shame (rather than hide it and allow it to fester), is important. When you acknowledge the existence of specific painful emotions related to shame, this acceptance immediately diminishes the power the emotion has over you and greatly influences how you relate to and react to the shame).

Failing to acknowledge (experience) shame and express it in a healthy way can lead to anger, self-deception, self-blame, and other personal vulnerabilities such as pessimism (negative self-talk), desensitization to feelings (overlooking your feelings), and other negative behavioral patterns such as unhealthy lifestyle choices.

When you start owning up to shame, talking to it (and about it), and practicing awareness and self-compassion, you allow shame sentiments to dissipate. Shame is an emotion. Like most emotions, unless you welcome it and allow it full board, shame fades. By ruminating on shame, you allow it to fester and turn toxic.

Expressing your shame allows you to free yourself from its deathly embrace, and at the same time seek forgiveness from those whose standards you feel in violation of. Internalizing shame—in the form of negative self-talk and self-blame—is of no benefit to you or the people you interact with, including loved ones.

## **Action step**

Start owning up to your emotions—shame and guilt included. Hiding from something or denying its existence does not mean it will not affect you. Remember that with shame and guilt, the more you overlook them, the bigger and more influential in your life they become.

Instead of overlooking shame and guilt, experience and express the emotions. With shame, expression can be in the form of confiding in a trusted friend—or your therapist. With guilt, expression can be in the form of an apology and a change in behavior.

Next, we will discuss how to deal with toxic and unhealthy guilt.

# Chapter 6: How to Deal with Toxic, Unhealthy Guilt

When allowed to fester, which happens when we fail to do something about it, natural guilt turns into toxic guilt, the bad kind of guilt that leads to deep regret and shame.

Toxic guilt normally manifests as a pervasive sense of "feeling bad"—the experience is very similar to how we experience deep-rooted shame. This kind of guilt is often nonspecific, i.e. not directed at a specific thing or aspect, and will often leave you feeling deeply flawed, as if there is something inherently wrong with you or with your life.

Compared to natural guilt, dealing with toxic guilt is a bit more difficult and involved mainly because it involves dealing with behavioral and psychological patterns such as our self-beliefs.

Examined closely, it is easy to conclude that toxic guilt is a by-product of our reaction to stimulation within our environment. Feeling unworthy of forgiveness, or feeling that something you have done is so bad that it is irreparable, is one of the main causes of toxic guilt in its many manifestations.

## Step #5: Work With It

Dealing with toxic guilt and shame demands that we first learn how to work with it. By deciding to work with toxic guilt, which means recognizing it and then making the intention to do something about it, we effectively turn toxic guilt, a heavy burden to bear, into healthy guilt that we can use to bring about personal development, growth, and change.

Recognizing toxic guilt allows us to assuage the residual pain it causes. It also helps us deal with guilt as an accumulated feeling not as a character trait, a sense of being. When we recognize and accept our feelings of guilt, it becomes easier to pinpoint the exact transgression or mistake. With this awareness, it becomes easier to detach from the guilt—stop directing it at the self—to attach it to the mistake or transgression, and to take corrective measures for it.

On a psychological level, when we become aware of toxic guilt, it also becomes easier to recognize its negative thought patterns that lead to chronic stress and the negative, altered state that when experienced long enough, leads to deeper feelings of worthlessness (shame) and guilt.

At a top layer level, we experience toxic guilt in two forms: as part of our personality, a seemingly ingrained character trait, or as a subconscious feeling of 'feeling undeserving or unworthy' especially at specific times, or at a shallower level, as an external trigger such as when we make a grievous mistake or hurt someone deeply.

How we handle it is another reason why toxic guilt is so pervasive. Rather than do something about it, most of us are comfortable with lugging guilt around, as if it were some sort of badge of honor. When left to fester, guilt is very easy to activate. For instance, a fight with a partner over a specific element of the relationship can be a cause of cyclic guilt and problems.

A simple way to determine if you are carrying toxic guilt is to consider the nature of the various types of relationships you have in your life. If you experience a constant sense of "walking on eggshells," afraid of how your behaviors and actions will affect others, reflect on you, or reveal an aspect of your personality you would rather not reveal because it will bring about shame, it is possible you are carrying around toxic guilt.

Awareness is the first step towards downgrading toxic guilt into healthy guilt and then dealing with it in a healthy and appropriate manner. By cultivating your capability to be aware of your inner sense of being, it becomes easier to recognize the telltale signs of toxic guilt and shame and then to start doing something about it. We have already talked about how to cultivate awareness and identify your emotions/feelings.

How do you work with guilt?

## *Action step*

To work with guilt and shame, adopt a growth mindset. Instead of seeing your shortcomings and mistakes as pronouncements of your inherently 'flawed' nature, **choose** to view them as important lessons that help you become and do something differently the next time.

Additionally, become purposeful with your motivation and intention. Toxic shame and guilt are counterproductive and self-defeating; they overlook a fundamental trait of being human: failing and making mistakes. When you make mistakes, or when your actions fall short, rather than allow that to leave you feeling unworthy and remorseful, stop beating yourself up, and choose to do something about it. With shame, express it; with guilt, do something proactive.

What is the best way to deal with toxic guilt?

Toxic guilt tends to be cumulative, building from a specific transgression or sense of unrepaired hurt that influences and changes our belief systems and thought patterns. Toxic guilt especially develops from moments of deep pain, self-betrayal, and other factors such as neglect, feeling unwanted and unloved, or feeling as if you are failing yourself, which can lead to a form of free flowing, easy-to-trigger, pervasive guilt.

Other than developing a strong moral compass and holding yourself to a high enough set of values and standards, all of which make it easier to recognize the consequences of your behaviors and re-align them with your core values and standards, here are several steps whose implementation will help you downgrade toxic guilt to healthy guilt.

## Step #6: Practice detachment/separation

Guilt, shame, and worry feed on each other infinitely. To ease toxic guilt, and to some extent, intense shame, chronic worry, stress, and anxiety, it is important that you learn how to practice awareness—of the emotion—and separation, i.e. distinguish real guilt and anxiety from guilt and fear over what 'may' happen (a 'what if' kind of situation that fuels fear, guilt and shame).

Awareness allows you to realize when you are projecting our guilt—in the form of defensiveness—or shame. It allows you to focus on the actual happenstance, the actual act, rather than your perception of the guilt and shame-causing instance.

Awareness of the feeling and state of guilt (and shame in extension) also does another important thing: it stops the ruminative nature of our mind and emotions. Rumination is especially lethal because from it develops toxic shame and guilt that fester until they become unhealthy and capable of altering our self-image, beliefs, and perception.

Practicing awareness is relatively simple: simply practice mindful meditation and journaling.

### Action step

First, use journaling or meditation to become aware of your inner dialog especially in relation to your beliefs and value systems; negative self-talk leads to negative self-belief, feelings of shame and worthlessness, and in extreme cases, guilt over perceived shortcomings.

After becoming more aware of your inner dialog, start free form journaling where you pen down your thoughts especially those pertinent to specific sentiments that stir up your sense of guilt or shame. By journaling, you become more aware of your thought patterns, emotions, and feelings. With time, this continued awareness makes it easier to recognize the causative factors that trigger your sense of guilt, and then do something about it long before it festers and becomes toxic.

Awareness then leads to a desire for penance, the need to do something to make up for the wrongs we have committed. It allows us to see things differently, to practice detachment with our guilt, which simplified, means seeing our mistakes as just that, rectifiable mistakes instead of a pronouncement of our character flaws (a negative self-image).

By compartmentalizing our guilt, i.e. separating ourselves from the behaviors that trigger our sense of deep guilt, it becomes easier to manage guilt in a healthy way. Detachment makes it easier to accept guilt for what it is: a natural, human process.

# Step #7: Practice Acceptance

Resisting guilt is one of the main causes of toxic guilt. Defensiveness, a common guilt-adjacent character trait, is very prevalent in those with a deep sense of low self-esteem, shame, or guilt.

When we resist guilt and treat it as negative emotion, we tell our subconscious mind that it should treat it negatively, which it does by causing us to retreat into ourselves, the breeding ground of rumination, or to vent out our frustration on others by being harsh, rude, or uncompromising, the latter of which means a low sense of empathy. When we resist or overlook guilt, we give it more power. We allow it to fester and turn toxic.

Guilt is not something we should resist. Like most emotions, it is fleeting and its presence is communicative of a deep-seated desire to right wrongs or make things right. When you experience guilt of any sort, you have the option of inviting it in for a long or short stay.

When invited for a short stay and treated as a fleeting emotion, guilt is a positive emotion that leads to growth—such as action geared towards righting a wrong. On the other hand, when invited in for a longer stay, it leads to negative thought patterns, a negative self-image, and a perturbing, resistant, deep sense of shame and guilt.

### *Action step*

It is very important that you invite guilt for a very short stay and use it as a catalyst for change and growth. Start by becoming aware of when and why you feel guilty. When you do, perceive this sense as an indication of your deep sense of regret, and then actively do something that eases the sense of guilt, perhaps by offering a genuine apology and making some behavioral changes that ensure the hurtful behavior does not recur.

Accepting guilt means accepting it for what it is, a neutral emotion. When we welcome guilt (and shame) and allow it to fester, it takes on a negative element that limits our wellbeing. When we view it positively, as a message communicating a discrepancy in our values and beliefs and actions and behaviors, we treat it as an impetus for personal growth; even something as simple as saying you are sorry for a wrong committed is a great sign of personal growth.

Worth noting is that no matter how much guilt you "choose" to carry or the nature of the present circumstances brought on by the act or behavior that triggered your deep sense of guilt or shame, you cannot change the past. You can only make amends and take action that influences the present and future circumstances.

Irrespective of the nature of the happenstance, be genuine and sincere with yourself. Be honest about the cause of the mistakes—why you did what you did—how what you did hurt others, and more importantly, what you can do to make up for the mistake or error in judgment. Objectivity, accepting things as they are, is a strategic tool against toxic guilt.

# Step #8: Practice self-love

Dealing with both shame and guilt in a healthy way requires the practice of self-love, a desire to treat yourself kindly, as you would a dear friend. When you practice self-love, you practice what Sri Sri Ravi Shankar meant when he said, *"Find the love you seek, by first finding the love within yourself. Learn to rest in that place within you that is your true home."*

## *Action step*

The essence of self-love is to feel so kindly towards yourself that when you stare into the mirror, the reflection is that of someone you treat with love, understanding, and compassion.

# Step #9: Focus on action

When we do something shameful or something that leaves us feeling deeply guilty, we should focus less on our mess (or shameful act), and more on what we can do in the present to remedy the situation.

## *Action step*

Rather than concentrate on how "terrible you are," which as we have noted amounts to internal focus and self-blame, concentrate on "what you can do right now to make things better for others and for yourself."

Focusing on what you can do also limits the amount of rumination. Because guilt and shame both have an element of regret, when you focus on what you can do, say apologizing or acknowledging and expressing the shame, you shift your perspective to a healthier one.

## Step #10: Practice letting go and moving on

Out of all the strategies we have discussed, letting go (of both shame and guilt) and moving on, is the most effective. The process of overcoming shame and guilt is lengthy and there are instances where some forms of shame and guilt will be too pervasive to deal with using the strategies in this guide.

In such instances, other than seeking professional help when you need it, practicing letting go of things you cannot change or control is very effective—as noted in our discussions on existential guilt.

### *Action step*

If you have done all you can do to make restitution for a wrong, there is no need to beat yourself up; trust that even if the person in question does not forgive you, the effort is enough.

As variously mentioned, obsessing over both shame and guilt leads to rumination. Rumination makes it harder to let go of painful experiences or emotions. When you obsess rather than let go, your desire to hog emotions breeds a negative self-image that affects all areas of your personality, including your relationships and general wellbeing.

After confiding in a trusted friend, asking for forgiveness or making amends, letting it go, and trusting it will be enough, move on. Moving on allows you to stop beating yourself up or being a self-saboteur. It allows you to believe in doing your best and in your best being good enough.

# Conclusion

At the heart of all the strategies and steps we have discussed as a remedy for shame and guilt is the need to become aware enough to notice when healthy shame and guilt fester until they turn chronic, and out of this awareness, practice self-care, self-forgiveness and a desire to take reparative action and after which, letting go.

Doing this consistently allows you to change the narrative you tell yourself whenever shame and guilt occur. Since how you relate with your emotions is so important, when your relationship with shame and guilt is healthy, the results are a positive sense of self, someone capable of understanding the difference between "I am bad—shame—" and "I did something bad—guilt," the latter of which is easier to deal with in a healthy manner.

As you go about implementing the various steps and strategies we have discussed, keep in mind that doing so is a lengthy process, especially in instances where the shame or guilt has grown deep roots.

Be patient with yourself and should you need it, seek moral and professional support.

# Do You Like My Book & Approach To Publishing?

If you like my writing and style and would love the ease of learning literally everything you can get your hands on from Fantonpublishers.com, I'd really need you to do me either of the following favors.

## 1: First, I'd Love It If You Leave a Review of This Book on Amazon.

## 2: Check Out My Emotional Mastery Books

**Note:** This list may not represent all my Keto diet books. You can check the full list by visiting my author page.

Emotional Intelligence: The Mindfulness Guide To Mastering Your Emotions, Getting Ahead And Improving Your Life

Stress: The Psychology of Managing Pressure: Practical Strategies to turn Pressure into Positive Energy (5 Key Stress Techniques for Stress, Anxiety, and Depression Relief)

Failure Is Not The END: It Is An Emotional Gym: Complete Workout Plan On How To Build Your Emotional Muscle And Burning Down Anxiety To Become Emotionally Stronger, More Confident and Less Reactive

Subconscious Mind: Tame, Reprogram & Control Your Subconscious Mind To Transform Your Life

Body Language: Master Body Language: A Practical Guide to Understanding Nonverbal Communication and Improving Your Relationships

Shame and Guilt: Overcoming Shame and Guilt: Step By Step Guide On How to Overcome Shame and Guilt for Good

Anger Management: A Simple Guide on How to Deal with Anger

Get updates when we publish any book that will help you master your emotions: http://bit.ly/2fantonpubpersonaldevl

To get a list of all my other books, please fantonwriters.com, my author central or let me send you the list by requesting them below: http://bit.ly/2fantonpubnewbooks

## 3: Grab Some Freebies On Your Way Out; Giving Is Receiving, Right?

I gave you a complimentary book at the start of the book. If you are still interested, grab it here.

5 Pillar Life Transformation Checklist: http://bit.ly/2fantonfreebie

## PSS: Let Me Also Help You Save Some Money!

If you are a heavy reader, have you considered subscribing to Kindle Unlimited? You can read this and millions of other books for just $9.99 a month)! You can check it out by searching for Kindle Unlimited on Amazon!

Made in the USA
Monee, IL
07 September 2021

77541687R10042